MY POEMS ABOUT MY LIFE

In Rememberance of my Mom

ELVIRA GREER

Self Published

ISBN-13: 9781234567890
ISBN-10: 1477123456

Cover design by: Art Painter
Library of Congress Control Number: 2018675309
Printed in the United States of America

To my mom in Heaven.
CATHY JO FREY-BODLE
RIP-
JAN 29, 1970 TO AUG 26, 2015

PREFACE

These are poems from when I was really depressed and growing up. They are about me as a child.

"My mission in life is not merely to survive, but to thrive; and to do so with some passion, some compassion, some humor, and some style."

"Success is liking yourself, liking what you do, and liking how you do it."

"Courage is the most important of all virtues, because without courage, you cannot practice any of the other virtues consistently."

"There is no greater agony than bearing an untold story inside you."

"Hoping for the best, prepared for the worst, and unsurprised by anything in between."

"I love to see a young girl go out and grab the world by the lapels. Life's a bitch. You've got to go out and kick ass."

"If you don't like something, change it. If you can't change it, change your attitude. Don't complain."

"I do not trust people who don't love themselves and yet tell me, 'I love you.' There is an African saying which is: Be careful when a naked person offers you a shirt."

"I've learned that people will forget what you said, people will forget what you did, but people will never forget how you made them feel."

"You can only become truly accomplished at something you love. Don't make money your goal. Instead pursue the things you love doing and then do them so well that people can't take their eyes off of you."

"If you get, give. If you learn, teach."

"Be a rainbow in someone else's cloud.

"All my work, my life, everything I do is about survival, not just bare, awful, plodding survival, but survival with grace and faith. While one may encounter many defeats, one must not be defeated."

"I am grateful to have been loved and to be loved now and to be able to love, because that liberates. Love liberates. It doesn't just hold—that's ego. Love liberates. It doesn't bind. Love says, 'I love you. I love you if you're in China. I love you if you're across town. I love you if you're in Harlem. I love you. I would like to be near you. I'd like to have your arms around me. I'd like to hear your voice in my ear. But that's not possible now, so I love you. Go."

"You may shoot me with your words, you may cut me with your eyes, you may kill me with your hatefulness, but still, like air, I'll rise!"

DR. MAYA ANGELOU -RIP: APRIL 4, 1928-MAY 28, 2014

INTRODUCTION

About my life growing up.

CONTENTS

A PART OF ME

September 10, 2014

a part of me

September 10, 2014
I lost a part of me
Once a upon a time
'Cause I was wild and didn't want to let go
I didn't know I lost a part of me
Not until I was way out of hand
I lost a part of me
That is now finally coming back

AN INNOCENT CHILD

September 9, 2014

An Innocent Child
September 9, 2014

A young homeless child looking for a home but finds none
On the first day of school the mother's not around to comfort me
When I'm down-right scared
An innocent child of seventeen
I find myself locked up in a placement
An innocent child now afraid of time
Will I forget my goals and dreams?
I go to Maryhurst and meet people who care
I learn about peer pressure and much more
Now comes the time to break thru the....FEAR

DADDY, I NEED YOU NOW

September 10, 2014

Daddy, I need you now

September 10, 2014
Daddy, I need you now-
Please take me by the hand
Stand by me in my hour of need
Take time to understand
Take my hand daddy,
And lead me from this place
Chase away my doubts and fears
Wipe the tears from off my face
Daddy, I can not stand alone
I need your hand to hold
THE WARMTH OF YOUR GENTLE TOUCH
In my world that's gone so cold
Please be a daddy to me
And hold me day by day
Because with your hand in mine,
I know we'll find a way

Author notes

this poem is dedicated to my dad who wasn't in my life when I was growing up. he is finally trying to be a daddy to me

DARKNESS ALL AROUND

September 10, 2014

ELVIRA GREER

Darkness all around

September 10, 2014
Darkness, darkness all around me
I try to run but darkness follows me
Darkness, darkness, all around me
I tried to hide but it found me
Darkness, darkness, all around me
Reminding me that it wasn't meant to be

DARKNSS

September 10, 2014

Darkness

September 10, 2014
Darkness closes in on me suffocating me
Thoughts of self-harm and death are always on my mind
Nightmares and day-mares never seem to cease
Always there reminding me that it wasn't meant to be

FAKING IT

June 5, 2019

Faking it

June 5, 2019

Sometimes I feel like I am not wanted;

And that everyone will be better off if I am dead and gone; including my kids.

I have felt like this for a while now; and I don't think anyone's noticed.

I fake a smile, fake a laugh.

I don't know how much longer I can keep it up.

A lot of people say that they are there for me;

But when I really need someone no one is actually there.

I'm told that I am a "fighter" and I have that "fighter blood" in me;

But I think that the fight has done left me.....like everything else has.

HOW DO YOU KOW

August 27, 2018

How do you know

August 27, 2018How do you know if it's good or if it's bad?
How do you see the good in the bad?
How do you get where you're going from where you're at?
How do you know who's true and who's not?
Match made in Heaven let it be, but
How do you know?

LOVE

April 15, 2015

Love

April 15, 2015
Why does love hurt?
Does love always hurt?
Love is always around-
In the air; In my house;
In my school; In my family
Why does love hurt?

Author notes

this poem came to me when i had my heart broken by the guy i was
with and was hoping to marry someday

ME AND YOU

November 2, 2014

ELVIRA GREER

me and you

November 2, 2014
Roses are red
Violets are blue
The sun is beautiful so are you
Your eyes are so brown like the great brown earth
Your love for me is sweet like cake
My love for you never ends.

MY LOVE

September 10, 2014

my love

September 10, 2014

My love, my love; oh whom to give my love 2?
My love, my love; oh whom is worthy of my love?
This boy, that boy; oh whom to give my love to
Friend or foe, sister or bro?
My love, my love; Oh whom to give my love 2?

MY WORLD

September 9, 2014

My World

September 9, 2014

Ricky, my world, I'll love you forever and always
Ricky, my world, please don't go
Ricky, my world, please understand
Ricky, my world, please love me back

Author notes

this poem was written to my first born son who I gave up for adoption

NO MATTER

December 13, 2014

No Matter

December 13, 2014
No matter where I go or what I do,
It seems I can't get you off my mind.
No matter what I'm doing or who I'm with
All I think about is you.
You're on my mind when I'm with my family.
You're on my mind when I'm with my friends.
Taking care of cats or walking my dog you're on my mind.
Even when I'm with my man you're on my mind.
It seems no matter the time of day or what I'm doing you're on my mind.
Yesterday, today, tomorrow, every day you're on my mind.
Weather I'm with my kids, or with my friends, you're on my mind.
With my man or eating my ham, you're on my mind.
Will it ever be when you're not on my mind?
Every day, every night
Every waking moment, every sleeping dream
You're on my mind.

SLEEP

June 5, 2019

sleep

June 5, 2019
She sleeps at dawn or so they think.
She wakes in sweats not knowing where she is at.
She's flashing back to her rape.
Wishing it never happened.
Wishing these feelings of hate and anger would go away.
She's ready for healing.
Ready to be happy.
Sometimes she thinks it's never gonna come.
Some days she's so tired of life.
She thinks she'll be better off dead.
She has people who love and care about her;
So she fakes a smile, a laugh, but she's dying inside.

Author notes

I deal with depression. I am on meds for it.

STRANGE

July 5, 2018

Strange

July 5, 2018
It feels so strange how my heart beats a little faster when your near
It feels like I can't breathe when I'm around you.
I love you with everything that I am.
I am glad I have you.
You don't know how much you really mean to me
I'm happy when you're around me
You help me in ways that I can't explain.
Bobbi Jo Bodle
June 14th 2018

Author notes

I wrote this about my ex boyfriend Noah

THEY SAY, I SAY

August 27, 2018

ELVIRA GREER

They say, I say

September 10, 2014
They say I'm dumb
I say
I am fun
They say I'm stupid
I say
I know how to read
So
Don't judge me by my attitude
They say I'm ugly
I say
I am my own uniqueness
They say I'm not loved
I say
Stop being mean
Instead
I'm going onto college
To be smarter

WALKING ALONE

July 5, 2018

Walking Alone

July 5, 2018Walking alone along this lone depressed road called life in this big lonely world
Wishing I had you by my side walking with me thru it all
I don't know how I get by each day without you here by my side
I miss you every day and night
You were my best friend
I hated seeing you in pain, but you are in a better place
You were taken way to soon though.
Wishing that I could just pick up the phone and call you
Needing advice badly from you
I know you are up there looking down wishing you could be here for me
I just wish Heaven had visiting hours or a number
So, I could call or visit you
I know you are with me though
No matter where I am at or Where I go
I just must remind myself that
No matter what you are with me in my heart
So
I am not really walking alone along this lone depressed road called life
in this big lonely world.
Bobbi Settles
Tuesday, February 20, 2018

Author notes

I wrote this when I was really depressed as I just found out that I was pregnant by my rapist who at the time was also my roommate. This poem was kinda like a letter to my mom who passed away (RIP 01/29/1970-08/26/2015) who i always went to for advice

FEAR

July 5, 2018

fear

July 5, 2018
I fear that I'm falling for you hard
I fear that you will break my heart
As hard as I try
I can't keep the walls up
They just keep crumbling down
I don't wanna be hurt again
I don't wanna hurt you
I fear for me
I fear for you
I fear for us both
But
Especially you since you know that
I am falling for you hard

Author notes

I wrote this about my roommate (yes the one who raped me) before he raped me. he took advantage of knowing that I was falling in love with him.

WASNT MEANT TO BE

September 10, 2014

Wasn't meant to be

on September 10, 2014
I tried to be what you wanted,
But it wasn't meant to be
I tried to be the mother they needed,
But it wasn't meant to be
I tried to be her daughter,
But it wasn't meant to be
I tried to be the sister,
But it wasn't meant to be
Everything you needed,
But it wasn't meant to be
I'm sorry I'm not the one,
But it wasn't meant to be

WHERE TO GO

September 10, 2014

Where to go

September 10, 2014

Where to go when you want to run?
Where to go when you need to hide?
Where to go when the reminder comes back?
Where to go when it wasn't meant to be?

WHERE WERE YOU?

September 10, 2014

ELVIRA GREER

Where were you?

September 10, 2014
Where were you in my hour of need?
Where were you when the darkness came?
Where were you when it wasn't meant to be?

YOU MAKE ME SMILE

August 27, 2018

You make me smile

August 27, 2015
You make me smile when I'm with you,
Like no one has ever made me smile before
Your the best thing that's happened to me
I'm so glad I have you beside me
You are there when I need you
Your are the best that I have ever had
You are my true other half

Author notes

I wrote this about my ex husband Kevin the day after my mom has passed.

MEMORIES

September 10, 2014

ELVIRA GREER

Memories

September 10, 2014
No matter where I go,
They seem to always follow,
Memories of the past,
Which I wished stayed behind
It seems that they love to follow
No matter where I go
There's no sense in hiding,
Since they seem to know where I go
I might as well face the fact
That they are always going to follow
Even though I try to keep them far behind
They seem to be with me
Where ever I go
I might as well get used to the fact
That they are always going to follow
Or at least until I find a way
For the memories of my past to lead the way
So that for once
I will be able to follow on the path
That will lead me to a bright and happy future
Or I could try to forgive and forget
The people who have brought the memories to my life,
Even though that doesn't seem likely for me to do so

MY MOM

September 10, 2014

my mom

September 10, 2014
My mom is always there
To fill my every want and need
I couldn't ask for a better mom
To help me succeed
She doesn't like to see me hurt
'Cause it makes her really sad
She's very protective,
But I guess it comes with being a mom
My mom has that motherly touch,
That puts me to sleep every day and night
My mom isn't the old fashion mother,
'Cause she's really upbeat
I have fun with her all the time
'Cause shes the best mother anyone could have
She says I'm a sprouting image of her and I know I am
But that's a good thing since I wanna be just like her

Author notes

I wrote this poem about my mom who was and always will be my best friend. (RIP 01/29/1970-08/26/2015)

EPILOGUE

Lorem ipsum dolor sit amet, consectetur adipiscing elit, sed do eiusmod tempor incididunt ut labore et dolore magna aliqua. Ut enim ad minim veniam, quis nostrud exercitation ullamco laboris.

This is in laton which means: It is important to take care of the patient, to be followed by the patient, but it will happen at such a time that there is a lot of work and pain. For let me come to the smallest detail, who does not exercise any kind of work.

AFTERWORD

This book came to be due to how my life was growing up.

ACKNOWLEDGEMENT

I would like to thank everyone who kept at me to keep writing. I would like send a special thanks to my best friend/sister Jill Spanyer, My mom in Heaven, Cathy Bodle, and my boyfriend Alex. Thank you all for pushing me to keep writing.

ABOUT THE AUTHOR

Elvira Greer

I am 28 years old. I started writing to cope with my feelings and it just blossomed from there. I'm about to start on writing a book. i have 2 boys who's adopted out. I am currently going to college to get my bachelor's degree in vet tech.

BOOKS BY THIS AUTHOR

My Poems About My Life

This book is all the poems I have written so far about my life

Made in the USA
Columbia, SC
30 August 2022

66316708R00038